Islands in the Sun!

CORFU, SANTORINI, NAXOS, AND PAROS: BRIEF EXCURSIONS TO PAXOS, ANTIPAXOS, AND ANTIPAROS

GLYNN BAUGHER

iUniverse books may be ordered through booksellers or by contacting:

iUniverse
1663 Liberty Drive
Bloomington, IN 47403
www.iuniverse.com
844-349-9409

Because of the dynamic nature of the Internet, any web addresses or links contained in this book may have changed since publication and may no longer be valid. The views expressed in this work are solely those of the author and do not necessarily reflect the views of the publisher, and the publisher hereby disclaims any responsibility for them.

ISBN: 978-1-6632-4391-1 (sc)
ISBN: 978-1-6632-4393-5 (e)

Library of Congress Control Number: 2022915028

Print information available on the last page.

iUniverse rev. date: 08/18/2022

DEDICATION

I dedicate this book to my daughter April, son-in-law Jon, and granddaughter Veronica--great traveling companions for our two weeks together.

A special thank you to April, who did all of the hotel reservations--fine choices all--and the inter-island and return-to-Athens travel arrangements.

From the left, Veronica, April, Jon, and I at a favorite restaurant next to the Esplanade in Corfu Town.

PREFACE

Almost all of my immediate family vacationed at Smith Mountain Lake, near Roanoke, Virginia, in the summer of 2021. During that stay, my older daughter, April, suggested that it would be a good trip if her family of three and I traveled abroad the following summer. I suggested that we go to some Greek islands, for I had heard about them all of my life, had been to mainland Greece in 2019 on a college alumni tour, loving it; and they, though frequent travelers, had not been to Greece at all.

My younger daughter, Dawn, and her family did not seem inclined to go.

The general plan was that I would select the islands to visit, we would separately make our own travel arrangements over and back (for they live in California and I in Virginia), and April would make most of the reservations, at hotels and for inter-island travel. Much of this work was completed in late 2021.

The plans worked out despite my misfortune of breaking my left femur in a freak accident in February of 2022, an accident involving my cat Ricky, a dead field mouse, and my forgetting where I was on my spiral staircase as I went to get the dead critter.

I was also hampered by serious arthritis in both knees, but I thought that I might as well hobble with a cane around some Greek islands as around home.

This book is essentially my journal of that trip, with a few minor additions for clarity and history. Unless I am in the picture, all of the photographs were taken by me on that trip, lavishly illustrating the journey. All of the photographs were taken on my Google Pixel 6 Pro phone camera. I took with me my standard camera, a Nikon Coolpix, but soon gave up carrying it: The phone camera seemed to do as well and wasn't as burdensome to carry.

The cover photo is of the Liston, on the edge of Corfu Old Town. This arcade was built by the French in the early nineteenth century, modeled on the Rue de Rivoli in Paris. This action illustrates a part of the very mixed heritage of Corfu.

I got up at 3:45 a.m. so that I would have time to shower and shave, feed the cats, and make it to Tri-Cities Airport (Bristol, Johnson City, and Kingsport, Tennessee) by 5:30 for my first leg of the flights to Corfu, from Tri-Cities to Charlotte at 7:00 a.m. The original departure time had been a comfortable 10:30 or so, but then American Airlines changed it to an hour later, leaving only 40-some minutes to make the connection to O'Hare in Chicago, thence to London's Heathrow, with British Airways having a direct flight to Corfu. That was cutting it too close, so, leaving at 7:00 in the morning, I would have several hours in the Charlotte airport.

Daughter April, Jon, and Veronica left from California the day before, flying from California non-stop to Zurich, Switzerland (11 hours), arriving in Corfu on a direct flight from Zurich, to get there a day before me. That Greece is seven hours ahead of Eastern Daylight Time makes a loss of hours inevitable.

The Charlotte airport, as usual, was a madhouse, now the fifth busiest airport in the country. I had a 4-5 hour wait. Hobbling on a cane, I had a wheelchair assist in getting to my departure gate, thanks to my travel agent's arrangements.

After a slightly turbulent flight to O'Hare in Chicago (I know, I know, Greece is EAST of Virginia, but this was the shortest way from where I started), I had another wait, this time about 2 1/2 hours, before departure for a 6 1/2-hour flight to London.

We got to Heathrow about 6:30 a.m. British time, finding the best assistance yet, needed for my walking with a cane. The Heathrow worker helping me said that they are not allowed to take tips.

I took a bus transfer way out to Terminal 5 for the flight to Corfu, finding an attentive section of the terminal labeled "Assistance." We accumulated several dozen people while I was there for a good while. A bit past 8 a.m. I was wheeled by a very capable man, Indian- or Pakistani-Briton, I think. Heathrow everywhere evinced its title as world's busiest airport. I've never seen so many masses of people traveling, and this was at an auxiliary terminal. My wheelchair pusher was so skillful and helpful, especially in expediting our way through security, that I tipped him 30 British pounds that I had gotten back home, along with euros, to be ready. He had acknowledged that he could accept tips. On presenting my boarding pass, I found that the woman told me I had been "offloaded" since I was so late appearing. My throat tightening, I told her that I had left "Assistance" exactly when told. The courteous woman got on the phone and got me "onloaded" again, and my attendant--I'm sorry that I did not get his name--pushed me to the plane's very door.

A very gracious English flight attendant took my two bags, and I was among the first to board the crowded airbus, with three seats on either side of the aisle. I have had aisle seats throughout my trip, because of the "assistance" label, I assume. My seatmates were a British couple who fly to Corfu fairly often, for her sister, married to a Greek man, has a home on Corfu.

The flight to Corfu took about three hours. As we deplaned at the airport, I found that we had the stair-kind of exit. The lovely flight attendant took my bags down and handed me over to a young man, also apparently English, who got me quickly through the lines. I was startled to see that my passport was checked, not by an airline official, but by a man in a policeman's uniform.

On my own, I made my way outside the airport to the stand where April had pre-booked a taxi service to my hotel, less than two miles away, I guess. I was the sole passenger on a Mercedes mini-bus.

Corfu is often said to be an atypical Greek island, unlike dozens of others. I would say from my brief experience that this statement is true. In Homer's *Odyssey,* Corfu, known to the Greeks as Kerkyra, is the last stop on the long journey of Odysseus back home to Ithaka, another island in the Ionian group. Before and after Odysseus, Corfu has attracted the nations and been occupied by them over its long history--the Romans, the Venetians, Napoleon (who obsessed about Corfu) and the French, the British. All have left their mark, unlike in most other Greek islands.

Corfu gets more rain and is therefore more verdant than anywhere else in Greece. In the 1930s the Durrell family of England settled here and grew to love it as their home. I'm ready for its lush variety.

My hotel, the Bella Venezia, earlier, when it was located in the Liston downtown, the Grand Hotel d'Angleterre et Belle Venise, is very fine, the outside an orangey-pink stucco, a former mansion, dating from the late 19th century. This mansion, one of many on Zambeli Street in Corfu Town, is the only one to have survived the brutal Nazi bombing of Corfu in 1943. I'm glad it did.

The Bella Venezia, fronting on N. Zambeli Street.

The back of the hotel, photo taken from next to the breakfast pergola.

Once I got the desk attendant, Spyros Nikolaou, to show me how to work things, I had fine air conditioning and a shower. A very nice young man who covered the hotel's bar and general duties, Alexandros Dapergolas, his name tag saying only "Alexander," had taken my bags up in the small elevator to the third floor, second floor in British terminology, the entry floor labeled 0 in the elevator. I tipped Alexandros 10 euros despite his shy demurs.

April, Jon, and Veronica are at a beach hotel about a mile away, where they can swim, snorkel, parasail, and windsurf.

Once refreshed, I walked out heading for the nearby Old Town. I still had on a long-sleeved shirt from the frigid planes and was much too hot. I took pictures of the appealing old place, full of tavernas and restaurants the way I walked, on Guilford Street.

On my way to Corfu Old Town, this photo of balconies and ironwork shows French influence, one of the many architectural styles of this island.

Town Hall, the first floor built of local white marble by the Venetians in the 17ᵗʰ century. The Venetian Republic ruled Corfu for four centuries.

I bought a juice box and hobbled on. I saw the edge of the Old Town, and took off my long-sleeved shirt. On the way back to the hotel, I met a young man taking a photo of a dazzling purple bougainvillea that I was also photographing. Finding that he had nearly perfect English, I asked him if he knew what the flower was. He did not and welcomed the information. Surprisingly, he was an Iranian who lives in France. Jon said later that he must know at least three languages well--Farsi, French, and English. We talked about 15 minutes, he surprised that I had loved both my profession--college teaching--***and*** retirement.

I made my way, slowly indeed, quite hot, back to the hotel. [Later, I was to discover that the other islands were much cooler and breezier than Corfu, or that Corfu was having unusual heat.] Somewhat later April, Jon, and Veronica came by my hotel to see whether I wanted to go on a walking and culinary tour with them that evening. I needed a long nap and to recoup otherwise.

Before that, I needed a little something to eat. As I left the hotel, I saw a woman, perhaps an artist, loading what appeared to be canvases into her small car. She greeted me, and I described to her what I wanted and asked her if there was any source of just sandwiches nearby. She said,

"Come with me," and escorted me up the steps back into the hotel. Like a Corfiot Aunt Dahlia talking to Bertie Wooster, she started talking to Spyros in very voluble and what sounded like authoritative Greek. Judging by its outcome, I would say that her harangue was to tell Spyros what he must do. As soon as she went back to her car, Spyros asked me what kind of sandwich(es) I wanted and got on the phone.

I got Spyros to order me chicken souvlaki sandwiches on pita bread (two for them to deliver), two for 7 euros. I tipped the very young delivery guy 3 euros, and he smiled hugely. I got a Coke over ice from the hotel's bar, and Julia, the serene, young, comely waitress connected with the hotel's bar, brought it out to me in the side garden. I ended up chatting with a couple at the next table about the English language. They had been working on a word puzzle. The English are obviously one of Corfu's largest tourist groups.

The lobby of this fine hotel. Alexandros is at the elevator door, and Erika, I think, and Spyros are behind the desk, just the top of the head of Spyros visible.

I went to take a "nap" and slept until 11 p.m. Greek time and then was quite awake for most of the rest of the night.

I went to breakfast, included in the hotel rental, a bit after 7:30, right after service opened. The breakfast room, with indoor and outdoor tables, is in a beautiful setting, the outdoor tables, where I ate, in the shade of a huge pergola covered in bougainvillea, wisteria, and trumpet vine, the largest-trunked wisteria I've ever seen.

Part of the indoor and outdoor breakfast areas at Bella Venezia.

A waitress helped me with my tray of excellent food--a huge array of choices. I got a cheese-stuffed croissant, toasted wheat bread, eggs (with the orangest yolks I've ever seen) over medium, with limp English-style bacon, fresh-squeezed orange juice, black tea with Greek honey and a bit of milk, pineapple juice, butter and orange marmalade, and a small bowl of fresh sweet cherries. A splendid breakfast in a beautiful garden setting.

My second breakfast at Bella Venezia.

Two facts about life in the Greek islands every book, article, and commentary we had read made clear: All drinking water has to be bottled water, for the water from the faucets is not reliably potable; and one does not put toilet tissue in the toilet to flush: the plumbing pipes are of such small diameter and water so scarce (the tradeoff for cerulean, cloudless skies every day this time of year) that this practice is a necessity. Putting the tissue in a closed bin soon becomes habitual, and the bins are cleaned every day.

Covid was apparently a big problem in the Greek islands as in much of Europe. Especially on planes and in crowded venues a number of people still wore masks, but most did not, and we did not. Jon was talking with a Corfiot health care worker, complaining about how the refusal of so many Americans to get vaccinated vitiated the effort to fight the virus. The Greek woman said that the same was true in Corfu, with a good number of people anti-vaccines. She had dealt with one young man who said that he would not take the shots, for he didn't want to ruin his ancient Greek DNA!

Today, I took a taxi to Old Town. One gets the hotel desk attendant to call for a taxi, and it is there quite quickly. The cost to the older part of Corfu Town was 10 euros, but when I returned to the hotel later, it cost 5 euros. As elsewhere, everything seems to be rounded to a nice figure--no $4.99 charges. We all found out later how short a walk it was to Old Town if we went down the hill from my hotel, to the waterfront and turned left. We did it, quite comfortably even for me, once April's family moved to a hotel about a hundred yards or so downhill from the Bella Venezia.

*At the southern end of the Esplanade, just down a hundred yards or so from my
hotel, stands the Maitland Rotunda, honoring the much-disliked first British Lord
High Commissioner of Corfu after it became a British Protectorate in 1814.*

The Old Fortress, built in the 16th century, as viewed from the Garitsa Bay area. The classical building is the Church of St. George, built in the mid-19th century so that British soldiers would have a place of worship.

I had the taxi drop me off at one end of the Liston, a long, long arcade modeled on the Rue de Rivoli in Paris. I walked slowly in the heat and took photos as I rambled. I spent much of my time in the outwardly not very handsome Palace of St. Michael and St. George. It is extremely opulent indoors, with state rooms and the furniture quite luxurious.

A state room at the Palace of St. Michael and St. George, built by the British in the early 19th century.

Another state room at the palace.

And another state room at the Palace.

Grand staircase at the Palace.

I don't know why, but Corfu doesn't seem to have as many signs and directions in English as the rest of Greece, and I had a bit of trouble finding my way to the Museum of Asian Arts, housed in this Palace. I approached a couple to ask directions, querying whether they spoke English. It was my favorite comeback of the trip, for the woman said, "Of course we speak English: we're German." But they gave me incorrect directions, to another art gallery than the one I sought.

The Museum of Asian Arts has a wide sweep of arts, everything from a 19th-century Japanese ceramic cricket cage to the armor of a Samurai, from Indian erotic carvings to Baluchistan carpets. I stayed a long time, took many photographs, and felt that I had more than used up my 3-euro entrance fee. The riches are so many that it is impossible to show but a small sample. I will confine myself to what I found the best display, the Japanese arts, with one item from a surprisingly strong exhibit of Uzbekistani art, mostly textiles. But the Palace was under-air conditioned, and it was a relief to get back outside.

A ceramic cricket cage, Japanese, 19th century, in the Museum of Asian Arts, in the Palace of St. Michael and St. George.

Noh theater masks, the Museum of Asian Art.

Japanese tea room, the Museum.

Japanese combs and other dressing items.

From Uzbekistan, a woman's light coat.

I sat at one of the long, long series of restaurants along the Liston and had a refreshing ginger beer and the potato chips that came with it. The drink, not found elsewhere in the Greek islands, as far as I could discover, is an adopted taste, like cricket, from the fifty years of British rule of Corfu, 1814-1864. Then the British--and this is an anomaly--voluntarily withdrew its imperial presence as Modern Greece became a state, including Corfu.

I saw some striking churches and observed some sea-bathers, but was about ready to take a break. Near the Old Fortress, a church built in the 16th century stands out. And the most famous church in Corfu, that of St. Spyridon, who died in the 4th century, whose mummified corpse in its silver casket is carried through the streets of Corfu Town four times a year, is the tallest on the whole island.

The Church of Panagia Mandrakina, built in the mid-16th century.

Sea-bathing, as the British call it, in St. Nicholas Bay, off the end of Corfu Old Town.

The Church of St. Spyridon, with the highest belfry on Corfu. What appears to be specks on the camera are the omnipresent birds, swallows I suppose, eating insects.

I took a quick taxi back to the hotel, realizing as the taxi drove back that my hotel is quite close to the sea. After a refreshing shower and a short nap, I walked down to the water and took a number of photos, buying a cold ginger beer [They're addictive.] at a little shop across from my hotel.

Corfu Town has a clever series of one-way streets, but they are often narrow, choked with cars and many, many motorbikes and motor scooters. The best I can tell, gasoline here is now over 10 euros per gallon, sold by the liter. Some scooters, quite a few really, are electric, approaching silently, so one has to be alert, for scooters go where you would think only pedestrians belong. I've seen only one electric car, a Tesla Model 3, parked in front of my hotel. Many cars are banged and dented, with scarcely six inches between two cars for parking.

Most of the cars I see are very small, most quite unwashed. I have seen a one-seater Honda and a one-seater Toyota, neither ever seen before.

April, Jon, Veronica, and I are going out to dinner. I waited for them in the hotel's back garden; we talked a good deal. Alexandros, on behalf of the hotel, recommended a restaurant, the Taverna Barbas, just a few hundred yards from my hotel. I found out later, from a chat we had on Facebook, that he is a vegetarian and would not have sent us to a restaurant that served meat, had he a choice.

We had a table outside in a side street. It was an excellent restaurant. Jon and I both got fried grouper, which the waiter, perhaps one of the owners, brought out to our table, with several other fish, before it was cooked. It was served with boiled vegetables. Veronica ordered shrimp and pasta, and April a fancy salad. We ordered a number of sharables, mostly appetizers and salads--fried feta, cheese wrapped in phyllo with honey and sesame seeds; grilled sliced vegetables and mushroom slices, and a really good traditional Greek salad, one "serving" doing for four people, almost exactly the size served for four people on mainland Greece in 2019. Jon got a beer and, later, a Coke over ice; I had a lemon ginger beer over ice, much stronger than the previous ones I had; and we had still and sparkling water throughout. At meal's end, we had a complimentary plate of deliciously ripe watermelon and honeydew.

April fed one of the ubiquitous wandering cats the remnants of the fish and shrimp. It was an excellent meal, costing over 140 euros for the four of us.

I am now Facebook friends with Spyros. He seemed to want to see my posted pictures of the hotel, all of them and the remarks quite flattering, for I am very well pleased with Bella Venezia. Alexandros also became my friend on Facebook. A sweet young man with many interests, he may not respond much after the beginning.

Today I spent most of the day on my own while April's family frolicked at the beach.

I started out from the Liston, wanting to find the shop devoted to Durrelliana. Much walking, but I found it, a tiny bookstore with a young woman from mainland Greece presiding. I forgot to take even one photo. We talked for a good fraction of an hour, she telling me the taxi rates (75 euros) for a trip to Kalami, where the Durrells lived, and Lawrence continued to live, I think, the rest of his life. His house, called the White House, is still there and sometimes open to the public. This is the setting of his book *Prospero's Cell.* He called the beach there "perhaps the most beautiful in the world." I decided to give up the idea of a trip to Kalami and slowly made my way through the crowded, narrow streets of the shopping district on a wiltingly hot day. So our stay on Corfu was to be devoted altogether to Corfu Town.

I stopped at a restaurant--and it's my guess that Corfu Town has more per capita than any other place I've ever been--and got a Coke, sold in the small bottles still, over ice. It came with a slice of lime, costing 3 euros, which seems to be the default price for every potable sold in a cafe. After sitting at the restaurant a good while, I started walking again, going probably no more than 100 yards before spying a shop/restaurant that sold Kri-Kri ice cream, the brand that friend Martha and I had so enjoyed on Poros, I think it was, in 2019. I got my favorite, pistachio, which nut grows all over the Saronic island to the north of Poros, Aegina.

I was sort of looking for a birthday present for April, her birthday tomorrow, but saw nothing appropriate. Gold- and silver-plated leaves and flowers with no price tags represented the kind of thing I found. However, I bought myself a very small table runner, handmade in Greece, to put under flower arrangements for dinner parties.

When I came out of the shopping district, I found myself not at the Liston but walking diagonally, exiting right near the "New" Fortress. Hot and tired, I got a taxi back to my hotel and took a nap after cooling down in the air conditioning.

The "New" Fortress was built later in the 16ᵗʰ century than the "Old" Fortress.

April's family had moved from their beach hotel to a large one a few hundred yards just down the hill from the Bella Venezia. We walked toward Old Town Corfu and settled on a fine, fine choice of a restaurant, next to the Esplanade but not opposite the Liston, where almost every food was oven-grilled. Jon ordered grilled chicken with bearnaise sauce, Veronica "water buffalo" burgers (not sure what the quotes mean) and a broccoli salad, April an asparagus dish, and I grilled haloumi cheese on bread with tomato and a sauce; with a coleslaw with apples and walnuts, dressed in a yogurt and mayonnaise sauce; and a grilled potato with butter, sour cream, and chives. We had a nice-sized boule of dark bread, wonderfully good, still warm. We had much food sharing, the servings very large, and cleaning of the olive-wood platters on which the food was served.

The delicious boule of dark bread that came with our meal.

The very personable young waitress said that since I ate the last particle of food I would be the first to get married. I told her, "Not likely at 78." She either was amazed or pretended to be, saying that she would have guessed that I was around 60. Very gratifying to hear, even if it was meant as the grossest flattery. Her English was very good. She said that they had to study it in school and that she actually preferred English to Greek, finding it so much easier.

We walked slowly home, the others escorting me essentially to my hotel before walking down an alley a short way to theirs.

I got up early (with the assist of a wakeup call in addition to my cell phone alarm) to walk down to the bus stop to go to the ferry excursion to Paxos and Antipaxos, more or less an all-day trip. I could have had a quick breakfast but was afraid to, the bus departing at 8:15. April's family hotel being quite close to the bus stop, I beat them there nevertheless.

The entry to the picturesque alley leading up from near April's family's hotel to mine.

The small bus took us and a whole load of passengers to the harbor, where two large ferry boats, both nearly full, loaded us efficiently. The ferries had only minor kinds of food and lots of drinks, not very cold. I got, of all things, a small can of Pepsi to take my morning pills. I soon moved to a shadier location as the seat selection opened up.

Jon shot this picture of me on my camera on the ferry as we progressed down the length of Corfu.

It seemed to take an extremely long time to traverse the Ionian Sea down the length of Corfu. The ferry stopped at a second Corfu harbor, Lefkimmi, near the southern tip of the island, to take on some more passengers. April's family had found shady seats on the second deck's sides, riding sideways, the prow of the vessel to our left. Very nice, except for some passengers, the young women in bikinis or other very revealing swimsuits, with only a thong between their buttocks, spending most of their time parading from the prow of the vessel to the bar, to the restrooms, to visit others.

With very little space to walk in, they were back and forth, back and forth, their derrieres, or, more crudely, their almost totally naked asses, right in my face. I felt like I should have been entitled to trip at least five or six of the most constant exhibitionistic wiggleworms.

The ferry steered into the "Blue Cave" of Paxos and allowed time for a good bit of picture-taking before backing out. It also steered into a few other rock formations on the wild coast, reminding me of the caves on the unsettled portions of the Isle of Capri, Italy.

A cave on Paxos.

A sizable rock in the sea off Paxos.

Docking in Lakka harbor on Paxos, we had a bit more than an hour and a half. April and I walked to a restaurant in the harbor, while Jon and Veronica swam there.

At the restaurant I ordered fish and chips, April just a drink. The food was good but weird, the fish cut in two slices perpendicular to the spine and deep fried, the potatoes fried in wedges. A soulful-eyed black dog begged for a bit at our table, but he belonged to the owners of the restaurant. The man, who had more English than his wife, said not to give him any food, that the vet forbade it.

While we were there, a hefty couple, almost swamping their little boat, which looked made of plastic, though it had an outboard motor, docked and went to buy some groceries before wafting off again toward home.

Buying a bag of fruit for 3 euros at a market for Jon and Veronica, April ate some with them while I bought a red raspberry sorbet at a Häagen-Dazs ice cream shop with few choices.

Back on the ferry, we resumed our seats on the mostly shady side of the ferry, noting that it would remain the shady side when we turned around to go back north in the late afternoon.

The ship anchored in a cove with picturesque rock formations and blue, blue water so that the passengers could swim for an hour. This was Antipaxos, with scarcely any habitations visible on this part of the island.

Daring divers--mostly very young men and women--started diving off the third deck, sending up torrents of spray as they whomped into the water. We had observed small jellyfish and schools of small fish beforehand. Jon went swimming and snorkeling and April and Veronica just swimming. Veronica may have dived off the second deck of the ferry, but I didn't see her.

Swimming off the coast of Antipaxos, with its swirly rock formations.

I had foolhardily brought my journal, thinking I would catch up on writing when I knew that we would be gone all day, but I was not at all moved to do so. The water, the sea breezes, the sunshine--all were entrancing.

On the way back, which seemed quicker, Jon and I mostly talked about Greece and world affairs. I knew a few things from my Emory and Henry alumni tour of 2019, and Jon is a wide reader, especially caught up just then in some of the idiocies of established religions.

We made it home, our bus driver being solicitous, as all drivers here--taxi and otherwise--to make things easier for me on my cane, to drop me off as close to my hotel as possible, just a piece of a block away, the others getting off with me.

After refreshing ourselves, April and I walked to Old Town in search of a simple dinner, say sandwiches. Jon and Veronica had gone to get gyros, but I don't especially like them. We found a good place, and Jon and Veronica joined us to add to the gyros they had already had. Everyone got sandwiches, salads, or similar fare, April, as always when possible, sneaking food to cats, this time a battered old white-and-gray warrior. She carries a small box of dry cat food in her backpack and rattles the box to attract them when she doesn't have our leftovers.

We noticed on Corfu (and this was to be true on Santorini also but not much on the other islands) a large number of mixed-race couples. Many of them, and I admit to guessing a good deal here, seemed to be British, unexpected in an earlier age.

A quiet walk back home brought us to our hotels.

• •

April and I were taking one taxi to the Corfu airport, Jon and Veronica another, so that there would be room for their luggage. Since April wanted to leave before 8, I ate a hurried breakfast at Bella Venezia. Goodbyes, to Spyros and Alexandros especially, to Konstandina, Erika, George, and Julia, were bittersweet. I had written a glowing review in their guest book. I promised to send Spyros (and, via him, George) pictures of my Maserati when I got home, since they are both big fans.

Since there seem to be no direct flights from Corfu to Santorini, an 8-hour ferry ride away in the Kyklades, we had to go to Athens, with a two-hour layover there. Both the Corfu airport and Athens were madhouses. We had to check our main bags because of the nature of our tickets, no charge, on a smaller Aegean plane. In the Athens airport, we sat, nibbled, and drank before we had to go to the departure gate, a great jumble of people. Most of these smaller flights mount movable staircases, one at each end of the plane, for the long and crowded airbuses.

Our taxi from the Santorini airport drove us through the constant, frenzied traffic of Fira, the capital of what the Greeks have in the past called the island of Thira. The name "Santorini," named for Saint Irene, comes from the time when the Venetian Republic ruled some of these islands. It ruled Corfu for 400 years, and we see lots of Venetian architecture in Corfu Town.

Our taxi got us quite close to our hotel, the Aria Lito Mansion, where I had a suite for one--a bedroom, a hall, a sitting room, a small wet bar, and a bathroom. It was elegant (and expensive), quite convenient for what we wanted to see and--thank goodness for me with my acrophobia--not on the cliffs of the volcanic caldera. Hard to understand why so many people live on the very edges there, but there's not a great deal of room elsewhere.

The Aria Lito Mansion, our hotel in Santorini.

View from near my door at Aria Lito.

The traffic on the main street below our hotel, maybe a half-block down the hill, is quite constant, all of the big trucks (for instance, gasoline trucks) and a number of travel vans and buses being Mercedes-Benz.

Our first night in Fira, we ate at an Italian restaurant with spectacular views, all of the paths around the cliff tops having steps, steps, steps, uphill from our hotel. Santorini is thought by many to be the Atlantis that Plato speaks of, its past inhabitants clearly having had a volcanic explosion and a tsunami to deal with, but--unlike Pompeii--apparently knowing beforehand long enough to flee. Unlike at Pompeii, no corpses have ever been found in digging through the ruins.

A huge ship on the waters of the volcanic caldera as night comes on.

Our hotel has elegant breakfasts outdoors, dominated by a trumpet vine on a pergola. But it is a wasteful breakfast, containing far too much food for most couples to eat. I liked choosing my own foods at the Bella Venezia in Corfu better. Our trays always included large bottles of water to take back to our rooms' fridges.

A breakfast at Aria Lito.

April did what she could to carry some surplus food to give to a begging woman with a young child up the steps toward the Catholic Church of John the Baptist. She seemed especially grateful for anything one gave her.

• •

I went out by myself the first morning in Santorini, walking slowly, taking random photos of a blue-and-white Fira, Santorini. I think that I absorbed a lot of this place.

That afternoon, April had booked a photo tour via a small bus/van, just the four of us with the driver Christos, which he insisted on simplifying to Chris for us. An affable fellow with pretty good English, he talked almost incessantly, cheerfully ignoring my list of where I had said we wanted to go on the tour. He apparently does the tour his way, and had ignored many a Chinese list bigger than mine.

The van/bus was a three-rowed Fiat. Seated on the right of the second row of seats (no door on the left), I had trouble stepping up into the high van, entering with my injured leg, but Chris added lifting help each time.

Chris was determined that we see the highest point in Santorini, on the island's southern end, at Akrotiri. The hairpin turns and gut-churning cliffs got to me at least a bit, but the view of the caldera was spectacular. One could see that volcanic eruptions had shaped this island in the distant past.

Chris took this shot of us near the top of the highest point on Santorini, the volcanic caldera at our backs.

Chris also drove us to some other favorite spots in the southern part of the island--to a black beach, volcanic sand with chunks of white pumice, a boardwalk running the length of the beach. Later we walked over rough terrain to see a "red" beach. Chris seemed to think I shouldn't go, but I did. The terrain was often rather desolate. Chris said that it looked like the surface of the moon. Later, he drove us to a lighthouse, not very special but with a great view of the caldera and ships of all kinds out on the water.

Black beach, of volcanic sand.

Veronica, with April and Jon behind her, next to the "moonscape" of this volcanic island.

Everywhere, on the most desolate, dryest, and stoniest ground, grow little grape vines almost right on the earth, with no support except that the canes are woven into a basket shape. The grapes, then with clusters of small green fruit, are used to make a beloved Greek white wine. The DNA of the grapes, many centuries old, seems to have adjusted to the severe conditions and survived when a great many European grapes were wiped out by diseases in the 19th century.

Ancient basket-woven Santorini grapes.

Toward day's end, Chris drove us to the north end of the island to one place we had requested visiting, Oia, pronounced [EE.a], renowned for its splendid sunsets. But this day's sunset was a fizzle. Many blue-and-white, the domes always blue, Greek Orthodox churches here--the ones we most often see pictured. The town is very crowded, very touristy, and pricey, still easier to get around than Fira.

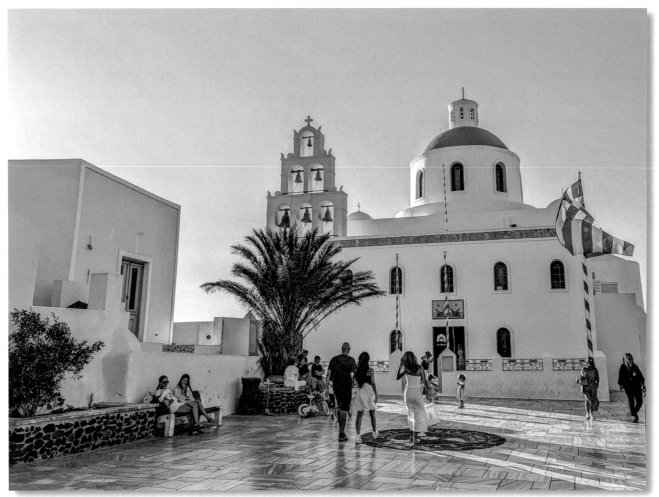

Typical blue-domed Greek Orthodox church, Oia.

We ate at a restaurant that seemed way overpriced to me and not very good. Jon got a hamburger for 25 euros! I ordered crab salad and did not like it, but Jon and Veronica, quite the omnivores both, polished it off, and April liked her food.

We caught a small bus back to Fira, a longish way, pleased with paying only 10 euros each. April's phone had helped us a great deal in navigating Oia and finding the bus.

After breakfast, I went up the steps above our hotel, slowly browsing my way, heading toward the Catholic Church of St. John the Baptist. On the way I stopped at a shop/gallery of unique wood carvings and other arts, mostly the work of an Albanian emigré to Santorini, Eduart Gjopalaj. I was sorely tempted and thought I might go back to buy something. Quite close, on the other side of the steps, I quickly purchased a woven tapestry in rich colors, on special offer for 15 euros, and a table runner at the same price. I paid for them, agreeing with the saleswoman that she would remove the wooden pieces at the top and bottom of the tapestry, so that I could get it into my luggage, and hold the two items until I came back later to collect.

The Catholic church with the beautiful campanile was quite winning and welcoming, a glory of dazzling blue under the main dome.

The campanile of the Catholic Church of St. John the Baptist.

Outside the entry to St. John.

The main dome of St. John.

St. John.

I went down the many steps parallel to the caldera's cliffs and then turned left toward the hotel again. In a miscellaneous shop I bought four vinyl placemats depicting Oia and one of the most-often-seen blue-domed churches. I got five bags of cooking herbs to take back to Martha.

On the way down the interminable steps, I saw the beggar woman with a young child that April had taken food to. I gave her all of my pocket change, a better deal with euros, for that currency has coins for both one and two euros. Jon had given likewise to another beggar playing music near the Italian restaurant. Santorini, and, later, Paros had the only beggars we were to see on our tour. I saw none in Corfu or in Naxos.

I went back to the art shop and bought Martha a pretty little piece, a ceramic sea urchin. Then I decided, hang the cost, I had to have a distinctive carving, of mahogany, iroko, and meranti woods, a picture carved, a beautiful image of a young man with eyes closed, emerging from the varied carved cubes. The surround features black volcanic sand. I don't think I've ever paid so much for an art work before--450 euros, with shipping costs to the USA of 100 euros more.

Sculpture by Eduart Gjopalaj, self-taught sculptor, an Albanian emigré working and living in Santorini.

Then I picked up my two items from the shop across from the gallery and went back to my hotel. The response when I posted a picture of the carving on Facebook was gratifying, praise such as "stunning," "amazing," and "beautiful" in chorus, with "Wow" icons a-plenty.

My bathroom at this expensive hotel, about double what the others cost, is not very good. The water is very slow to heat, and then the shower has to be monitored closely, for the temperature rises to scalding all at once. The shower is over in a deep old bathtub whose sides I could barely clear with my bum leg. My last morning there, I took a sponge bath in the sink, afraid of injuring myself in the challenging shower.

The receptionist got a plumber friend to come fix my sink that leaked quite a bit underneath, and then that was good. One morning I had shaved in the sink in the wet bar to avoid a wet floor.

In the afternoon I worked a bit on my journal and may have dozed out by the swimming pool for a while. Since April's family left for a catamaran trip on the caldera, I ate a late lunch of spanakopita and a pistachio milkshake at an eclectic cafe up the stairs and to the left.

I returned to the same cafe as it neared dark and the family not back. I ate lightly, a baguette sandwich of ham, turkey, lettuce, and tomato with a Sprite over ice. Coca-Cola seems to have a monopoly on soft drinks in the islands, also featuring pretty good canned ice tea.

As I was leaving the cafe, an English man and woman, he a self-employed electrician, started a conversation. They were from Lincolnshire, had visited America several times, and he especially loved country music, like his mother before him. He mentioned especially Jim Reeves, Marty Robbins, and Hank Williams. I told him he must watch the Hank Williams biopic *I Saw the Light*, with his countryman Tom Hiddleston playing Hank, doing his own singing, quite well, of Hank's songs.

Leaving Santorini for the ferry to Naxos, we found that our taxi, a small bus, was late, using the standard explanation in Fira that he was stuck in traffic. April kept phoning, though there was no problem, not really, in not being at the ferry harbor at least an hour in advance. There were perhaps eight people total on the little van/bus taxi. To get to the harbor, the vehicle had to go a distance out from Fira and wind down hairpin turns and switchbacks to go down, down, down to the water.

What prodigious amounts of work were required to build this road, which wound through cut rock and switchbacks. On the way we saw laborers, sweating mightily, building a wall of large stone, one man hammering away at the stone without any eye protection. April had gotten the ferry tickets at the station in Fira, 60 euros per person for the passage, which seemed high for the distance, airline tickets to Athens costing only 40-some euros.

The harbor was an absolutely jam-packed horror show--literally thousands of travellers for this huge ferry and dozens of cars, this ferry one of at least a half dozen a day, with stops at Ios, Naxos, Mykonos, perhaps Paros (I don't remember), Syros, and eventually Piraeus, the port for Athens. Thus the crowds.

Not knowing how things worked, we stood jam-packed for an hour through the building to Gate 4, with the line, about 10 or more people abreast, stretched out yard after yard after yard behind us.

When the huge Sea Jet ferry arrived, it disgorged a mob, thousands of people almost running and a few dozen cars, people surging down the gangplank at least ten abreast, for Santorini. Then a dozen cars or more drove onto the ferry, and the multitudes followed, others carrying one of my bags and I struggling to keep up.

We stowed our bags on a rack in the steamy lower level, where the cars were, and worked our way up the intentionally narrow stairs, where only two people could emerge at a time, having our tickets scanned, while the ferry was already racing away from the harbor. We emerged into a new world, luxury airline type seating but with far more space. Our assigned seats were toward the back, in Row 75, with at least 12 feet of space in front of our section, with a descending stairway to our left and women's restrooms to the right. The others quickly found empty seats behind us and stronger air conditioning at the back of the huge, huge vessel. I stayed put and people-watched.

It was about an hour and a half trip, much longer than I expected, from Santorini to Naxos, still in the Kyklades. I was used to seeing the island group called, after the Roman spelling, the Cyclades and used to saying SIGH.cla.dees. But of course the Greek alphabet has no C, using kappas for the spelling of a sharp K sound. It makes more sense to transliterate the name with Ks. I heard a Greek man say the name of the islands, and he said kee.KLAH.dees, Kyklades. Santorini and Mykonos, both in the Kyklades, annually take in a huge portion of Greece's gross income. For decades now, Mykonos has been well known as gay-friendly, party central for those who want a vivid nightlife in their vacation spots.

Our landing port was Chora, or Naxos Old Town, on the west coast of the island, but we were headed to our hotel, just about two blocks from the sea, in a section called Agios Georgios (St. George), which was signposted and labeled on maps as "St. George Beach." Our taxi driver was speeding away, although it soon became apparent that he didn't know where our hotel was. April showed him the map on her phone, and he did almost a 360-degree turn and brought us to the hotel, I think going the wrong way on the one-way street.

The hotel is ultra-modern, quite imaginatively decorated, the Villa Flora, for as we found out later the owner is named Flora Latina. She did the decorating and later told me that it was an ongoing project, that she had already spent 100,000 euros on getting the hotel going. Flora was not there at the time when we arrived, but the woman of all work, quite genial, had our keys ready. She served us big glasses of orange juice and a good lemon cake, but she seemed not to have a single word of English.

I have a large, queen-sized, I suppose, but it seems larger, bed. The floors are all marble, much marble being quarried on both Naxos and Paros, often called the marble isles. Indeed, Parian marble has been valued for fine sculptures through the ages. The Venus de Milo and the Hermes of Praxiteles, which we saw in Olympia in 2019, are of Parian marble.

Naxos harbor, with the castle that dates from the 13th century near the town's top.

The Villa Flora, St. George, Naxos.

My balcony, Villa Flora.

The seating in my room and Flora's decoration, the Villa Flora.

Three large tree trunk sections, two of them sculpted somewhat, quite decorative, are used in my room as occasional tables. I have a small balcony with a marble-topped table and two wrought-iron chairs, with a retractable clothes dryer behind me. [Most clothes drying here seems to be open air, the eternal sunshine and low humidity making that ideal.]

I have a marble shower stall with perfect water temperature and a window to open to let out the steam, though it has no overhead stationary shower head yet, just a handheld shower wand. Three snippy young women that checked out before me commented adversely in rating the hotel. Flora was quite hurt at their mean-spirited review and told me that she was working toward getting full shower heads.

In the late afternoon Jon and I walked about town. We are immediately liking this place, so much quieter, more laid-back, and relaxing than Santorini. There are plenty of visitors to provide livelihoods for the locals, but it seems relaxed, less expensive, greener. The hotel is nicely placed, with many good restaurants and two small markets just an easy walk away, and the beach very close. April's family had gone swimming in the sea, the Aegean, already. We saw the first cemetery we had seen in the islands.

Breakfast seating, Villa Flora.

St. George Beach.

Cemetery, St. George.

April found us, and Veronica now napping and planning to eat later, we sat for dinner at a harvest-to-table restaurant. April had a huge salad with strawberry dressing, Jon a plate of mussels followed by fried chicken pieces. I got a grilled chicken fillet, accompanied by fried potatoes and a dish of slices of carrot and zucchini.

As dark drew down, we returned to the hotel. I decided to catch up a bit in my journal writing.

After breakfast at the hotel, with lots of homemade pastries but enough protein and really good watermelon and other fruit, I did a long walkabout, first to the beach and then all around, taking dozens of photos of typical or, paradoxically, odd items that struck my fancy. Agios Georgios is a pleasant, clean, winning town. I posted 25 or so of the pictures on Facebook.

I mostly rested during the middle of the day, having bought some chocolate milk--the first I have had in donkey's years--red plums, and a wedge of watermelon to take back to my room's little fridge. I washed out in the sink a few pair of underwear and socks with body gel and hung them on the retractable clothes line on the balcony, using the few clothespins available. Then I sat on the balcony, ate some of my treats, and fiddled with my phone.

I napped a good while. Since April's family were going on a rather long walking tour to the old castle and environs--too challenging, I thought, for my leg, knees, and walking cane, I went to eat dinner at a seafood restaurant about two blocks from my hotel.

I had grilled sea bass, a very good, buttery baked potato, with a small salad on the platter, dressed with oil and vinegar, with a can (by Coca-Cola) of lemon iced tea. Most people in the islands don't seem to eat dinner before 8 p.m., so the restaurant grew busier and busier as I sat. It was a fine, simple dinner and experience.

Fish meal, St. George, restaurant near our hotel.

I went to bed shortly after 10 p.m. after checking out television for the first time on this trip. Very few choices, the clearest being the BBC World News, but I wasn't in the mood for talking heads.

After breakfast all four of us took a taxi, the driver a friend of Flora's that she called for us, with a big, luxurious Mercedes, to the harbor and market center of town to get my ferry ticket to Paros, for the time after April's family left from Naxos for Athens and the return to California. A day or two ago I noticed an oversight: I had no hotel, either on Naxos or Paros, for July 3 but was scheduled to leave Naxos on the third. So April asked about my staying an extra day at our hotel, the Villa Flora, and I paid Flora this morning.

While getting the ferry ticket to Paros, we also arranged for me to take a tour of the rest of Naxos, a photo tour usually requiring two customers at 50 euros each for the tour to go. I was the only one signed up and wanted the tour, so I ponied up 90 euros for a private tour of the island.

While there in the town center, we walked through the charming alleyways of the market section and through the old castle. I photographed the Catholic church inside the castle, and then we went to a nice restaurant on the roof, with a panoramic view of the town. At the restaurant, I just had a glass of wonderfully refreshing sour cherry juice, which seems to be available on the islands in general. On the way to a taxi stand, I bought an attractive pashmina with a Greek motif that I plan to use as a table runner.

Alleyway in the shopping district, Chora.

I posted on Facebook some pictures in the afternoon that I had taken that morning. My fine phone camera makes posting while abroad quite easy (though I discovered later that I was paying much more for phone service than usual, because of the posting, I assume; I scarcely used the phone otherwise).

For dinner we walked a few blocks from the hotel and ate well again. I had grilled pork tenderloin, lemon potatoes, and a small salad with pomegranate seeds and a vinaigrette dressing.

Arts at a shop, Chora

Veronica was sleepy, and since they leave at 7 a.m. from the hotel tomorrow morning, I hugged and thanked Veronica for her help. (Among other items, she had cleared my phone of an annoying PIN required to open it.) It was good to see her for almost two weeks. April and Jon and I sat a good deal longer at the restaurant, ate some complimentary watermelon, and left as space was growing scarce at the restaurant.

We said our goodbyes downstairs in the hotel, April arranging the details of my flight and hotel in Athens until the last minute. Their living in California means that I don't see them as often as I'd like.

• •

April, Jon, and Veronica left for the Naxos airport at 7:00 this morning, in the Mercedes taxi of Flora's friend, the same one who drove us to the port yesterday. They will fly to Athens and see some of that city today, and then tomorrow, on July 4th, will fly to Zurich, and thence home to California.

We said our goodbyes last night, but I went out onto my balcony shortly before 7 to wave and bid them Bon Voyage.

Today, I am to be picked up at 10:00 at the hotel to go on a private photo tour of Naxos. Tomorrow I have a 9:50 ferry to catch for Paros, where I will stay for a bit more than two days before flying from the Parikia airport, to stay overnight at a hotel near the Athens airport, flying out July 7th, Athens to London to Charlotte to Tri-Cities.

The tour guide, Panos, was 20 minutes late to the Villa Flora hotel, saying that he couldn't find it. I saw no evidence of a cell phone on him. But he gave me an extra hour, six hours instead of five, at day's end. I was surprised to find that our transport was an older car, a banger, as the Irish say, a red Daihatsu of indeterminable age. But Panos was very fond of it, praising its reliability. He is a middle-aged guy, a photographer some twenty years.

I was a bit further ill at ease when Panos stopped at a service station and added a liter of oil. I queried, "It's using oil?" and he said, "Olive oil." The front seat, where I sat, was quite low, rather difficult for me to get into with my bum leg. But Panos was patient and helpful.

He drove the stick shift well, with real authority, downshifting as we descended the mountainous roads. We drove a good distance, right out into a sparsely settled rural area. Our first stop was at the ruins and museum of a temple of Demeter, the agricultural goddess. The walk to the temple remains from where Panos parked was somewhat long and uneven, the paving stones anchored in gravel. But we took our time.

The way to the Temple of Demeter.

There is evidence here that this was a site for worship and offerings to Demeter from the eighth century B.C., and the elaborate temple, mostly of marble, that is modeled in the museum dates from the 6ᵗʰ century B.C. The temple was turned into a Christian church in the 6ᵗʰ century A.D., during the reign of the Roman emperor Justinian.

Model of the Temple of Demeter.

A few ruins and modern reconstruction of a small part of the Temple of Demeter.

Fierce Aegean wind blew the whole time we were there, even fiercer on the hilltop where the temple's few remains, with some newer work to give a visual idea of the building, stand. Panos seems to be well-informed on herbs of every kind, though he focused more on health than cooking as he broke off sprigs of wild oregano, with its pretty thistly lavender-pink blooms, thyme, rosemary, bay leaves, basil, and so on, always urging me, "Smell, smell."

Entry to the site of the temple and the museum was 4 euros, but Panos did not have to pay. Everyone at the sites we visited seems to know him well. When we were arranging the tour, the ticket agent on the phone with Panos made it clear that one site usually featured, a cave deep in the mountains, would have to be stricken from the list.

Wisely, I photographed the information on placards along with the ruins, the information--as nearly always in Greece--in Greek first and then in English, and only those two languages. The museum had much information and lots of artifacts, such as parts of columns, pieces from the Christian church, ironware, and so on.

On the way to the next stop I had Panos stop for a moment as I photographed the first extensive vegetable garden I had seen in the islands. It was behind a stone wall and clearly irrigated with drip piping. A luxuriant garden of vegetables and greens was a delight to see.

An irrigated garden on Naxos.

Next we drove to nearby Sangri (or Sagri, road signs spelling it both ways) and walked an easy ten minutes on sandy, mostly flat ground, unpaved. All around were sheep and goats, but I saw no cows. Restaurants boast of having Naxian milk and butter.

We crossed a dry river bed, lined with sycamore or plane trees. Panos said that it is a good river in winter. Just on the other side of the almost totally dry river was an idyllic scene: a constantly running fountain of potable water with maidenhair ferns around. Panos splashed the water all over his face and drank big gulps, so I did the same. He said the water came from higher up in the mountains. The mountains appeared to be as dry as the landscape lower down.

The ever-flowing fountain of Naxos.

Then we saw what Panos called the "world's oldest living olive tree," which he says has been officially dated at 5,000 years, dated from a thin section of one of its roots, the root system running all around, with descendant trees from those roots. I think that the claim is disputed by advocates of other, handsomer trees but there seems to be evidence that Panos is right: the tree is between 5,000 and 6,000 years old.

The olive tree.

Close by, as we went along a little path toward a Greek Orthodox chapel, we saw a luxuriant mulberry tree, with some ripe fruit well within reach. A French couple there, with very little English and apparently no Greek, did not know mulberries. As I ate a few, the woman did also. We would see them later, at an olive oil press.

Opening the dragging wooden door of the windowless chapel, Panos lit a candle. He's Greek Orthodox, crossing himself as a matter of respect every time we pass a church.

I am seeing more pickup trucks here in Naxos, both in town and country, than I've seen elsewhere in the islands. The French couple, leaving just before us from the parking area, were traveling in a pickup. I saw no sign of its being rented.

Next we visited two interesting home factories--a pottery manufacturer with a huge kiln for curing the pots. Panos just called it an oven. A fat chicken sat at the doorway with her owner, watching me insouciantly. She made not a sound even when my cane, ever the drama queen, threw itself on the stone floor.

Some works of the home pottery factory. On the top shelf are figurines inspired by the early Cycladic figures made of marble, some dating from the third millennium B. C. Modern artists like Henry Moore have been inspired by the Cycladic pieces.

Other work of the pottery.

As insouciant, and handsome, a chicken as I've seen.

Our next stop was at an olive press, with a giant screw and a large rotating wheel to grind the olives. We found the French couple here. Panos cheerfully wrapped ropes around his shoulders and pushed the working mechanisms of the olive press to demonstrate how it was done. The information placard on the wall said that the olive press was 1850 years old! I don't know whether this exact wheel and screw were meant, or just this operation.

The wheel that crushes the olives, human-powered.

The olive screw, for pressing the oil from the crushed olives.

Next we stopped in Halki or Chalki. All of the maps and road signs have a C at the beginning of the word, its name in Greek apparently beginning with a chi, but Panos seemed to insist it began with an h, though I think maybe he was explaining the initial sound of the name.

The main street of Chalki is unprepossessing, but we stopped at a cafe where Panos knows the owner. Panos ordered a dessert for both of us, a kind of custardy square made from the cafe owner's own farm's eggs and milk. It had a stultifyingly sweet sugar syrup topping, I think sugar rather than honey, and I found it much too sweet for my taste, just like ordinary baklava, which I find overwhelming in its sweetness. Panos polished his off in record time, I more slowly, leaving some of the sugar syrup coating.

I relished my can of lemon tea over ice under the pergola made of steel rods and bamboo, which dripped with huge bunches of not-yet-ripe green grapes for the table, I assume.

Grapes above our head at the Chalki cafe.

The streets of Chalki off behind this cafe were charming. We stopped at a distillery in business since the 1890s and saw some interesting apparatus of the business--boilers, carboys, amphorae, and a machine for inserting corks in wine bottles. The distillery had samples of its wares and shelves full for customers to buy.

As we walked the back streets on our way back to the car, we saw an appealing little fruit market, an obviously well-loved and well-petted cat snoozing in the sun, and buildings with their balcony supports of stone still in place though the balconies were gone.

Boiler room of the 1890s distillery still in business.

Sun-dappled cafe in Chalki, Panos on the right.

A well-loved cat of Chalki.

On the way up the mountainside, Panos stopped so that I could take a picture of a village, Filoti, to the right. We then wound steadily upwards. It is a marvel to see the tremendous labors done in the past to create roads, walls, and so on in this harsh environment.

Filoti, a village in the Naxian mountains. The grayish trees are olives.

We drove to what seemed like a village on the mountain-top, Apiranthos ("many flowers"), seeing an old castle built in part on a huge natural rock. We also saw a formerly inhabited home of a wealthy family now kept on exhibit, with a peep-through front door. A bit further on, Panos pointed to a grape vine that had grown inside a house and then emerged a level or two above, through the wall, a hole cut for it, thriving again in the light. I asked Panos about a set of inscriptions beside an entry, blue lower-case Greek on the white paint. It was lovely to look at, but Panos glanced at it very slightly and said "Poetry" with a dismissive shrug. Panos talked for a while with a man he obviously knew well, while I sat and absorbed the scene.

Greek poetry at a doorway in Apiranthos.

A pottery, ceramics shop, Apiranthos.

A cool place to eat, Apiranthos.

On the way back down the mountain, the same route we took up it, Panos drove up to stop briefly at what he said was a still-working windmill, the Greek type that one sees quite often on these islands. There were no sails on its circles of spokes. There was no place to turn around, but Panos backed skillfully and confidently down the hill that would have given me palpitations to negotiate.

A typical Greek windmill.

It was an unconventional photo tour, and Panos, obviously having done this tour many times, took just a couple of photos. Finding out early that I didn't really want or need instruction, he let me be, taking the pictures I wanted.

When we got back to the Villa Flora hotel, he wanted assurance that I was satisfied with the trip. I basically was "satisfied" but no more than that. I tipped him 20 euros and exited the Daihatsu.

Before bed, I readied everything for taking a ferry to Paros the next morning, with my taxi coming at 9 a.m., the same friend of Flora's that she had called for us several times. She says that he "is a good boy"--a boy in his 30s, it appears. He has always been on time and reliable for us. Breakfast at Flora's does not start until 8, but that's plenty of time.

As I left the Villa Flora, Flora said to me that my family and I had been ideal guests, that she wished all of her guests were as thoughtful. She complimented me on my family, I thought sincerely. She took a selfie of herself and me and later posted it on her Facebook page. I hugged her, well satisfied with our fine hotel.

My ferry ticket to Paros, I disturbingly noticed this morning, said that it was for July 3. Someone, I don't know just who, had made a mistake when we purchased the ticket on July 2. It cost 28 euros, and I expected a much shorter passage than that from Santorini to Naxos. The ferry was to be a fast one.

Still, delivered to the port, I had to try, not knowing how to correct the error. When the mobs of people started onto the ferry, early by my figuring, it did not occur to me that I was getting on not just on the wrong day but the wrong ferry. Strangers were helping me up the gangplank with my two bags, one with its handles looped over the towing bar of the suitcase.

A huge ferry at Naxos.

The harried man taking tickets was, understandably enough, quite rude, having to get me off the ferry without any wasted time. The ferries leave very quickly when people are aboard. I saw pity and concern in the eyes of some of the passengers, as I was near tears with frustration.

Still, a very nice young man working for the ferry company said "Sit here [on a bench that he gestured to] and we will make it right." I was supposed to have caught the high-speed ferry to Paros leaving 10-20 minutes later.

My ticket was accepted on this ferry without comment, though it was clearly for the day before. I suppose the young man had alerted the ticket-taker. The fairly short passage to Paros was unusually rocking, perhaps due to the ferry's speed. I was told to sit down--there were lots of empty seats--and exactly where did not matter. Implied was the phrase "before you fall down."

Inside the high-speed ferry to Paros.

Nearing the end of the trip, I heard my name called over the intercom, my last name only but pronounced clearly and correctly. I am not sure why I was called up just for the gentle man to tell me that they were accepting my ticket though it was for the wrong date. Whew!

So I arrived in the harbor of Parikia, the largest town and capital of Paros. After waiting a while for some of the people to clear out, I showed a taxi driver my hotel destination. He said,

"You're close; don't need a taxi" and gestured vaguely to the side. I have noticed how, harried by thousands of tourists, many officials are impatient with tourists' not knowing something that they have no way of knowing.

I found out, by asking a gaggle of teenaged girls, one of whom had enough English, the way to the Argonauta Hotel. She got on her phone and gestured the way. It was by then just 100 yards or so across a big public square, though not easy to see at first, for all of the rooms and the name are on the second floor.

The Argonauta Hotel, Parikia, Paros, all of the rooms on the second floor, though the outside breakfast and brunch restaurant and the lobby are on the first floor.

This was about 11 a.m., and I couldn't check in until noon, but a very helpful youngish man, Tassos, sent a teen-aged girl up to my room with my bags, there being no elevator, when my room was ready.

The girl was puppy-sitting, a really cute black Lab, for her uncle. Her grandmother came in to relieve Tassos at the desk. The girl, Stephane, was born in France, lived with her extended family for a long while in Oklahoma, speaking always at least Greek and English at home, using Greek and English by turns with her grandmother, who seemed to be keeping a watchful eye on our conversing. The grandmother seemed to relax and smiled at me when she learned that I am a retired college professor. Stephane and I talked mainly about languages, especially the vitality of English.

I am quite pleased with my room at the Argonauta, with marble, Parian, I suppose, all over, ultra-modern decor, especially in the bathroom, with a half-open space for the shower and a novel sink. The towels are by Guy LaRoche--impressive.

My shower and sink at the Argonauta.

Once settled in, with the air conditioning on 23 degrees Centigrade, acknowledging that the AC will not work if the doors are open (one set of doors to a very handsome narrow balcony) or the bathroom window. As in Naxos, the doors to the balcony can be opened a little, tilting forward for air, or swung wide.

Looking from my balcony at the Argonauta towards the sea at the end of the lane behind the hotel.

After a quick chicken tortilla and a soft drink for lunch at a place adjacent to the hotel, a bit annoyed by a man who was smoking at the next table, but who turned out to be quite nice, helping me to feed bits to a cat that seemed to have trouble chewing, I headed out to explore the fancy shopping streets near my hotel. It seems to be easier to find good places to eat close by in St. George, Naxos than here in Parikia, with lots more touristy shopping in the streets here. I bought a few things for the table, for dinner parties, though I surely do not need them. I spent a bit prodigally.

Shopping street in Parikia.

Another difference from Naxos: I saw no beggars where we were in Naxos, though we did see some beggars, both children and mothers with children, in Santorini. I see both here in Paros, though there are more children. Indeed, though they look middle class, I have seen two children who apparently are begging at their parents' orders. I saw the boy who begs while playing tunes on a small accordion turn money over to a man apparently his father while I got onto the ferry to Antiparos. And I saw a girl give the money she had begged to her mother, who was working in a restaurant.

I see a great many more smokers in Paros (and in Antiparos) than on the other islands visited. I have no theory why. People smoke freely in restaurants.

As in the rest of Greece, there are a great many stray cats and dogs roaming free, far more cats. The dogs look generally well-fed, and they just run through the edges of restaurants for what they can find on the ground, not begging. Many cats are reasonably well-fed but have to work hard if totally independent. They will beg, if only eye-beg, in restaurants. The restaurant workers seem to just ignore the cats and let them get on with it. April sneaked as much food as possible to these strays. I saw in Paros little handmade souvenirs, many of them depicting cats, that were for sale, with a sign that said, "All profits go to the stray cats of Paros."

I made a bad choice for dinner the first night--a traditional Mediterranean restaurant with an overworked waitress. I ordered grilled sardines, which were only so-so, with a bit of green salad and a cold drink.

I have grown addicted to milkshakes here, especially if I can find pistachio ones. They are pricier than in America, usually 7 euros. I can also find, at least on Naxos and Paros, sour cherry juice and drinks with sour cherry juice, both very refreshing over ice. I have found no ginger beer here as in Corfu.

Rather than write in my journal or do further research on what to see in Paros, I went to bed early tonight (and the next night also).

Up betimes, I had a refreshing shower and shave. I may have shaved every day while in the islands, which I certainly don't do at home in retirement. The breakfast/brunch at Argonauta is outstanding. One can order anything, as many things as one wants, from the set menu, included with the hotel charge. An excellent waitress and waiter attend, and I tipped them. The first morning I had poached eggs on toast as the main dish. The fresh-squeezed orange juice is the best I have had since Napflion in the Peloponnese in 2019.

Part of my first breakfast at the Argonauta.

After scrabbling around the harbor, I decided to take the 11:05 ferry to Antiparos, 7 euros each way, pay on board. When I got there well ahead, I found that the 11:05 ferry had been canceled, with no explanation why. So I wandered around for about an hour and a half.

A clever way to recycle the ubiquitous plastic bottles on the islands, this one on the sea front of Parikia.

Restaurants on the sea front of Parikia.

High up from the seafront, the Kastro, or castle of the medieval town of Paros,
now Parikia, still survives in part of this towering structure.

Serendipitously, I came upon the greatest ecclesiastical treasure of the Kyklades, the Greek Orthodox church Panaghia Ekatontapyliani ("Virgin Mary of the 100 Doors.") This is a magnificent church, said to be founded in the 4th century by Helen, the mother of Constantine the Great (after whom Constantinople is named). Most of today's form dates from the 6th century, the time of Emperor Justinian. One is puzzled where to look, such is the richness of decoration--the intricate carved woodwork, the hanging silver lanterns and chandeliers, the many, many icons. It is overwhelmingly magnificent, and I may have missed it altogether, but for the canceled ferry.

Inside the courtyard in front of the church. The gallery on the side appears to have been part of a monastery.

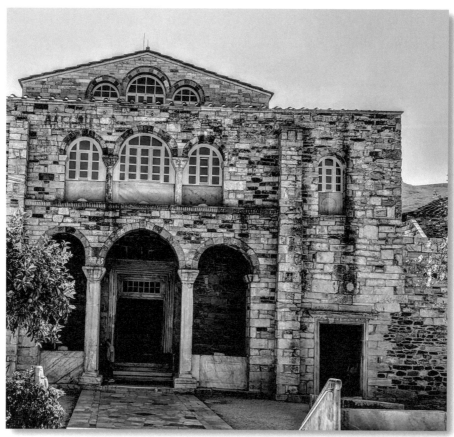

The handsome Byzantine front, main entrance of the church.

The left entrance of the church. The elaborate stonework of the arches and ceilings witnesses the involvement of the Emperor Justinian in the 6th century.

*This elaborately carved wooden piece serves, in part, to hold
the candles that worshippers light before icons.*

The central aisle of the church.

Looking to the left aisle.

Looking to the right aisle.

A particularly vengeful and violent angel in an icon.

The impressive domes of antiquity.

The ferry to Antiparos was bouncy, rocking from side to side, the waves stirred, I suppose, by the constant breeze/wind in these parts. Still, the trip was not bad, but the ferry was crowded, and right behind me was a young woman with an old person's voice. I know that she was speaking Greek, but it seems to me that her main language was inane gabble. Had I to swear in a court of law, I think that I could say she never paused for more than three seconds during the 25 minutes of our trip. The only thing that would have made the experience worse, I imagine, was if I had understood anything that she said.

Antiparos has been adopted by Hollywood as its home away from home, I hear, Tom Hanks and his wife, Rita Wilson, owning property here, and also Madonna. No doubt they are in villas up in the hills, not here in Antiparos Town, whose streets I walked for most of the 3 1/2 hours I had before the 4:00 return ferry I had decided to take rather than wait for the 6:00 one. I bought a couple of nectarines, a bottle of sour cherry drink, and, later, a ham-and-cheese omelet.

Handsome fruit stand outside a market in Antiparos, with a cat snoozing.

I walked, slowly, a great deal, snapping photos especially of the houses and businesses with striking decor. Every inch of the town seemed to be flawlessly paved and clean.

Bold and imaginative decor, a common factor almost everywhere
on the islands I visited but especially Antiparos.

Bougainvillea used well, Antiparos.

This handsome restaurant on Antiparos serves only dinner, starting at 6:30 p.m.

I bought a bag, which can be used for grocery-shopping, with "Antiparos" on it from a young woman who seemed totally uninterested in her job, and probably was.

I was one of the first people back on the ferry home and chose to sit at the back riding backwards for the gloriously fresh, spray-spattered rocking transit back to Paros. I took a clumsy video, not daring to stand up to make it better, and posted it on Facebook. We made it back to Paros in about 20 minutes.

I couldn't find a very good choice of restaurant around the harbor and just had a tuna baguette and a pistachio milkshake for dinner.

I see a great many rental cars, motorcycles, ATVs, and bicycles here on Paros. In addition, I have seen a number of adults on electric foot scooters. They push off as on a child's scooter, twist the handle, and are off, even middle-aged women in wedge heels.

It's good to see that the main street in front of the hotel is closed to traffic later in the day, the huge marble-and-granite square between the street and a fenced-in playground swarming with kids at play. Indeed, pedestrians predominate, tourists mainly, I suppose, even when the street is open.

I see a large variety of cars on Paros. On Naxos, Fiats seem to have had a near-monopoly on the car-rental business. I wonder whether there have ever been any Greek-made cars. I haven't seen any and know of none. I see cars from all over, most compact but surprisingly large Skodas, from Czechoslovakia, part of the Volkswagen group now, I understand, and lots of French cars. Citroens of the small sort don't stand out as so odd-looking these days. The only Parikia police cars I've seen are Peugeots and Kias.

I packed my suitcase and bag well, for I fly to Athens tomorrow at 7:10 p.m., leaving a gap between checkout, at 11 a.m., and leaving time. Storing my baggage in the hotel lobby will, I know, be no problem. To bed early.

After a large breakfast, I readied to check out well before 11 a.m. Tassos brought my bags down, to stay here in the hotel lobby until around 5:30, and booked me a taxi to pick me up for the airport at 5:45.

I catch the taxi at the end of the little lane behind the hotel, perhaps a hundred yards or so, opposite the bus station. Tassos says that he will ask the young woman at the hotel desk then to help me carry my bags to the taxi.

Another breakfast at the Argonauta, including rice pudding.

I wandered around much of the day, foot weary, seeing the old Frankish fort that dominates the waterfront, buying a gift for Martha, talking at a restaurant (on Burger Street!) to a nice couple from South Africa now living south of Los Angeles. They said that when they first came to the islands, perhaps a dozen years ago, there were almost no signs in English and very few people who spoke English. The Greeks now apparently see how much their economy depends on tourism, and how tourists often know English even when it's not their first language. Students appear to study English, perhaps as a requirement, at school.

Part of the Frankish Fort on the seafront, made of parts of even older buildings.

A pomegranate tree, the fruit not yet ripe, in Parikia.

I spent a good part of the afternoon in the Argonauta lobby catching up my journal. Strange how fitful journal-writing is, sometimes the furthest thing from my desire, sometimes driving on at speed.

When it was time to go meet my taxi, the young woman at the desk, and I'm sorry that I did not get her name, took both of my bags and walked me to the taxi stand. She would not let me carry anything. Tassos had certainly taken good care of me, and I've met such care almost everywhere.

I crossed the road to the bus station to wait for my taxi, judging that that was the correct side of the road to the airport. It came a few minutes later, a woman driver in a large Skoda. She had two people--friends or family?--in the back seat and told me to sit up front. The taxi seemed as luxurious as the Mercedes-Benz taxis on Naxos.

An oddity I noticed was that the Skoda's dash had a big electronic date with the clock, the date given in American fashion, the month first, rather than in the European fashion, the day first. The taxi charged 25 euros for the long trip to the airport.

A great crowd waited at the small airport, for at least two flights were leaving soon, with only one departure gate and not enough seating inside the airport, or parking outside. Cars lined the road for quite a few yards. I sat outside for a good while, on the sidewalk, talking with a couple from Leesburg, Virginia, he a dentist but not a horseman, as one might expect of a Leesburger.

There was room to sit inside once an earlier flight left, and more room once we went through security. We were bused out to our Aegean flight to Athens somewhat later than scheduled but not outrageousy late.

After about a half hour flight we arrived at the Athens airport. Since my flight to London, via British Airways, is scheduled to leave at 8 a.m. April had booked me an overnight stay at the Aethon Airport Hotel, the hotel e-mailing me about the scheduled van pickup time at 2100 hours, giving me explicit instructions on where to meet the van to the hotel. Due to the lateness of my plane, the van had left and returned shortly before 10 p.m., picking up four passengers total, but only me for the Aethon. A very alert and helpful Greek man ran the connecting of airline passengers with the numerous pickup vans. He told me, "Sit there. They will be here, and I will tell you when they are."

I got to the hotel around 10:30 perhaps and asked about getting my boarding passes, three of them to go, whether the hotel had a printer. But I really did not understand what the desk attendant told me. She spoke English but so heavily accented I was having trouble. April, following my electronic trail from California, texted me but could not help. I asked for a wakeup call at 4:30 a.m. and the transfer van to the Athens airport around 5:30.

The hotel was ultra-modern and quite fine. I set my phone alarm but woke up just before it went off and just before the man who ran the late-night hotel desk knocked at the door--a real wakeup call.

When I got downstairs, this man was super-helpful, spoke better English than the woman who checked me in, and told me the van would be there in a few minutes to take me to the airport. Meanwhile, he talked to his well-fed, sassy cat and dog, telling the cat when she meowed at him, in English, "No, no! You have already been fed." I wondered whether the cat was bilingual.

I was the sole passenger in the van and sat up front with the driver, as he instructed me. He was a very affable, engaged young man with pretty good English. It was strange to see the busy Athens highways nearly deserted at this hour, the sun not up far. The driver drove me right to the section of the airport housing both British Airways and American Airlines, which often work together.

Since I was nearly out of euros and wanted to save some for tipping my expected wheelchair attendant around the Athens airport, I gave him my last 5 euro note and a $20 U.S. note, which he could get easily changed. He seemed thrilled to get a tip at all.

Inside, the British Airways counter was not open until 6 a.m. but I was second in line in my chosen lane, behind a family of an English-born mother and her two grown daughters and grown son. They live in Texas, Dallas I think, flying there at least. They were all well-educated, the three women, I think, already possessed of Master's degrees, the mother in art, the daughters in the sciences, the son, I would guess, still in college. They were great fun to talk to about education, the English language, the arts, and collecting (the young man).

I got a jewel of a British Airways employee, speaking a posh British accent and quite fluent in Greek when he had to get on the phone. He had me check my carry-on suitcase through, no charge, so I would have just a cloth bag to carry, with mostly dirty clothes and my toiletries. He got me all of my boarding passes. I had noticed before that all that was needful to get one's boarding passes was to get the counter person to scan one's passport. This action was new to me.

I had a wheelchair attendant, secured for all of my flights by my travel agent, to push me to the correct departure gate and help me through the security lines. I tipped him every bit of cash I still had left in euros, every last cent of it, between twenty and thirty euros.

The British Airways airbus left on time, taking about three hours from Athens to London.

Things went to hell when the plane landed at that maddest of all madhouses on this earth, Heathrow. When we deplaned, everyone else went to a bus that would take them to Terminal 3 for the next connecting flight. In its zeal to help (all I needed was a wheelchair to get to my departure gate in time), British Airways had sent a little van/bus for me, and the driver took me to Heathrow Assistance, Terminal 5, the death knell to my making my flight connection on time.

Inside Terminal 5 of the airport I was driven by a woman from Assistance who abandoned me--no other word will do--in the seats opposite British Airways, probably the maddest sub-madhouse at Heathrow. She took my now-useless boarding pass and passport to show someone and said that someone would come help me. No one did, as time dragged on, the British Airways wait lines growing to more than a hundred yards long, I would guess.

In a little room beside this wait line, labeled "British Airways Assistance" and "Iberia Assistance" my boarding pass for the 12:15 flight to Charlotte, now useless, was passed to the next assistant, who was soon replaced by a very skilled and helpful agent, Martin Till.

A young American couple before me, bound for Los Angeles, she severely handicapped, with one prosthetic leg below the knee, took two hours, I swear, to get their problem solved. When I got to the front of the line, I was prepared for another bout of long standing, leaning on my cane. But Mr. Till, my miracle-worker, had been working on my case during the long intervals of telephone holding while he solved the couple's dilemma.

He gave me boarding passes to Charlotte, same time July 8th, and from Charlotte to Tri-Cities, transit vouchers to and from a posh hotel, a free night at that hotel, with dinner and breakfast provided. Then he waited for me to go to the restroom and summoned an electric vehicle to take me and another passenger to the Terminal 5 bus stop to catch the H5B bus to a number of hotels.

My hotel, the Arora [sic] Renaissance, was the poshest I saw during the bus's stops. It is probably the largest hotel I've ever seen, with wonderful air conditioning, a lush bathroom, and a duvet on the bed.

My only complaint was that the bank of four elevators was hundreds of yards, it seemed, from my room, 3305. After a really good free dinner, entree grilled chicken, I decided to relax by watching the only television I had watched, beyond a minute, my entire trip. This was the day that Prime Minister Boris Johnson announced his resignation, so I switched to Wimbledon tennis, not needing to see Donald Trump Lite. I soon turned off the telly and fell asleep a bit after 8 p.m. English time, which would have been past 10 Greek time, my body now accustomed to it.

Friday, July 8

My sleep was erratic. Showered and shaved but dressed in yesterday's clothes, my suitcase having been checked and who knows where at the moment, I went to the hotel breakfast soon after it started, at 6 a.m. It was pretty good but not so good as dinner the night before. The night before, we had wine goblets for water; at breakfast we had paper cups to steep our English breakfast tea in.

I decided to catch the 7:30 H5B bus to Heathrow rather than sit around the hotel. I got to Heathrow around 8 a.m., knowing that I had to get to Terminal 3 rather than Terminal 5, where the bus delivered me.

Looking for help, I wandered onto a floor reserved for Heathrow employees apparently. Seeing my confusion and cane, a young man, apparently a Pakistani Englishman, came to help. He took me to the train that would take me to Terminal 3 [Yes, Heathrow is that big, needing trains and buses to get to some terminals.] and explained how the free ticket worked.

After a fair amount of walking once inside Terminal 3, I came to American Airlines, my flight to Charlotte at 12:15. Since I was there four hours before my flight, a "helpful" woman said that they would get me on an earlier flight, about two hours earlier. I was issued new boarding passes and then was apparently forgotten in the busy assistance area. I did not make it through security in time to catch that flight. No one is allowed through security within one hour of flight time.

I drew a whiz of a wheelchair pusher to attend me, an Indian man from Portuguese Goa who said that his name was "the Portuguese equivalent of Pedro," I kid you not.

Dealing with harried American Airlines people at Heathrow is not for the faint of heart. Nearing an agent, we were shunted to another one, the only total prick I had to deal with, a man named Richard, I think, who obviously believed that it was my fault that I missed my 10 o'clock flight. He started with a lie--that there were no more seats on my original flight, my 12:15 one that I had not asked to be changed from. Gradually "Pedro" and I wore him down with our pitifulness and obvious sincerity, and he grudgingly handed over, all at once, without comment or explanation, new boarding passes. I thanked the egregious ass unctuously, and Pedro wheeled me to security, with loads of time to spare. But this is Heathrow, with horrific lines always.

Pedro, bless his devious heart, was not above cutting corners, lifting ropes to get me closer to the security check when gabbling travelers did not advance the line fast enough to suit him.

Sitting in a wheelchair gave me the right to be body-frisked without arising from my seat, the friskers always asking for my permission to be frisked. Pedro took me to the waiting area from which I would be taken to my departure gate later. I tipped the man all of the British money I had--40 pounds--and he was thrilled.

Somewhat later, another man wheeled me to my departure gate, and I got to board the plane, a big Boeing 787, I'm pretty sure, first of all the mob waiting. The seats were three on the left, four in the middle, and three on the right in each row. By special accommodation I always had an aisle seat in big planes. The plane had the luxury of more toilets than most, with a light ahead to tell when the toilet was vacant. We had more leg room than on most planes, though the seats are still too narrow for full comfort. I suppose that fat people have to fly first class.

Planes get so cold in transatlantic flights, at 30,000 feet or so, that I was glad of my long-sleeved shirt and the individual blanket and little pillow at each seat.

The flight took a bit over eight hours, but we gained back the five hours lost on the flight to the U. K. We landed in Charlotte on time, and I was taken to my departure gate by a young man who, when we passed through security, saw my Maserati billfold that April had given me. He was impressed and told a friend, "He drives a Maserati!"

Unknown to Roberto--yes, an Italian name for an apparently young black man with dual American and Mexican citizenship [This is America!]--the departure gate had been changed. No problems, for I spotted it in time, and the plane for Tri-Cities was delayed in departing for over two hours due to severe thunderstorms in the Tri-Cities region.

When the pilots and the departure gate attendant, constantly on her cell phone checking the weather, had a flight plan, the dozen of us boarded a small plane, with one seat on the left and two on the right in each row. The flight, the pilot explained, which usually takes about 35 minutes, would take about three times that long, as he had to fly north of the Tri-Cities and go a long way around to dodge thunderstorms. Dodging thunderstorms sounded good to me.

We landed without incident at a nearly deserted Tri-Cities at about 9:30 p.m. I found my truck just where I thought I left it and paid my parking fee--over $153 for sixteen days plus--and got home about 10:20.

As I unlocked my front door, Sadie was right there to greet me, kitty curses on her lips. Ricky was cooler, so long as I fed him **at once**. In the following days he wanted to be fed six times a day, and Sadie wanted no more than 100% of my time, my attention, and my cuddles. The clinginess has not gone away yet.

It was a splendid trip--a world of sunshine, perpetually blue skies, sea breezes, and low humidity, a blue-and-white world of dazzlingly clear sea waters. In fourteen days in the Greek islands, I don't think I saw a single cloud.

Still, how good to be home! The work will wait. Life is good, and I had returned, physically unscathed, not much damaged mentally.

Printed in the United States
by Baker & Taylor Publisher Services